The Best Everton Football Chants Ever ...

The Best Everton Football Chants Ever ...

The Best *Everton* Football Chants Ever ...

and also the rudest

A Fan

The Best Everton Football Chants Ever ...

Unofficial and Unauthorised

All the chants in this book are common chants sung on the terrace during football matches, and are written here in a light hearted way they are not the thoughts and views of the authors.

Copyright © InterviewBooks.com
All rights reserved,
including the right of reproduction
in whole or in part in any form.

ISBN 978-0-557-19000-3

Designed and written by A Fan

The Best Everton Football Chants Ever ...

To all the Toffees fans out there, sing up for the lads!

The Best Everton Football Chants Ever ...

Contents

Introduction 9

1. Classic Chants 11

2. Everton Heroes Songs . . 17

3. Give them some stick . . . 25

4. The referees a w*nker . . 37

5. The Best Everton Websites . 41

6. Everton Supporters Clubs . . 45

The Best Everton Football Chants Ever ...

Introduction

Thank you for taking the time to read "The Best Everton Football Chants Ever ...". In this book we take a light hearted look at the popular chants, sung from the terrace each week.

Most of the chants sung from the terrace are sung in a light hearted way but are sung to provoke the players or fans from the other team.

This book covers all of the popular songs; no chant has been kept out of this book for being politically incorrect or too rude.

Get ready to have a laugh at the other teams' expense ...

Chapter 1

Classic Chants

The Best Everton Football Chants Ever ...

Chapter 1   -   Classic Chants

It's a Grand Old Team to play for,
And it's a Grand Old team to be,
And if you know your history,
It's enough to make your heart go woah,
We don't care what the Reds' fans say,
What the f*ck do we care
Because we only know,
That if there's gonna be a show,
When the Everton boys are there!
Everton, Everton, Everton!

Fight, fight, where ever you may be,
We are the famous E.F.C,
And we don't give a F**k,
Whoever you maybe,
For we are the famous E.F.C ...

Stand up if you love the blues,
Stand up if you love the blues,
Stand up if you love the blues ...

Oh when the blues,
(Oh when the blues),
Go marching in,
(Go marching in),
Oh when the blues go marching in,
I want to be in that number,
Oh when the blues go marching in ...

We are Everton
We are Everton
We are Everton
We are Everton

We're all going on a European tour,
A European tour,
A European tour

We're all going on a European tour,
A European tour,
A European tour ...

We love you Everton,
We do,
We love you Everton,
We do,
We love you Everton,
We do,
Oh Everton we love you

Hello, hello,
We are the Everton boys,
Hello, hello,
We are the Everton boys,
And if you are a Liverpool fan, surrender or you'll die,
Cos we all follow Everton ...

Everton till I die,
I'm Everton till I die,
I know I am,
I'm sure I am,
I'm Everton till I die

Come on Everton,
Come on Everton,
Come on Everton,
Come on Everton ...

(clap, clap, clap, clap, clap, clap clap)
Everton!
(clap, clap, clap, clap, clap, clap clap)
Everton!
(clap, clap, clap, clap, clap, clap clap)
Everton!

Come on you blues
Come on you blues
Come on you blues
Come on you blues

Chapter 2

Everton Heroes Songs

The Best Everton Football Chants Ever ...

Chapter 2 - *Everton Heroes Songs*

Follow, Follow, Follow,
Everton is the team to follow,
Cuz there's nobody better,
Than Mikel Arteta,
He's the best little Spaniard we know ...

Mikael Arteta
Mikael Arteta
Mikael Arteta
Mikael Arteta ...

Fellaini ni ni
He is over six foot three
Fellaini ni ni
He's better than Stevie G

In the air, on the floor,
Feed the Yak and he will score,
He is big, he is blue,
And he's coming after you ...

He's small
He's lean
He's Everton's number 3
Leighton Baines
Leighton Baines ...

USA, USA, USA, USA, USA ...
(Sung to Tim Howard)

Feed the yak
Feed the yak
Feed the yak, and he will score
Feed the yak and he will score

De, de, der, Victor Anichebe
De, de, der, Victor Anichebe
De, de, der, Victor Anichebe
De, de, der, Victor Anichebe ...

We bought the lad from Middlesbrourgh,
The Yak, The Yak,
He took his time but now he's shined,
The Yak, The Yak,
He's big he's blue he's 22,
He scored against them he'll score against you,
Who needs Torres when we've got Yakubu ...

Phil Neville,
Superstar,
He's got more medals than Steve Gerrard ...

Moyes, Moyes,
Davie Davie Moyes,
He's got red hair but we don't care,
Davie, Davie Moyes

There's only one David Moyes,
One David Moyes,
There's only one David Moyes ...

Were on the march with Moyes' army,
We're all going to Wembley,
And we'll really shake 'em up when we win the FA Cup,
Coz Everton are the greatest football team

Who put the ball in the red sh*tes net,
Who put the ball in the red sh*tes net,
Who put the ball in the red sh*tes net,
Super Kevin Campbell
Super, Super Kev
Super, Super Kev

Duncan is our hero, he wears the Number 9,
He wears his shirt with pride,
He wears it all the time.
He wears it in the shower,
He wears it in his nest,
Duncan is our hero,
He is the f**king best ...

The Best Everton Football Chants Ever ...

Chapter 3

Give them some stick

The Best Everton Football Chants Ever ...

Chapter 3   -   *Give them some stick*

When I was just a little boy,
I asked my mother what should I be,
Should I be Everton or should I be Liverpool,
Here's what she said to me,
Wash your mouth out son,
And fetch your fathers gun,
And shoot the red scum,
And shoot the red scum,
We hate Liverpool we hate Liverpool ...

Cheer up Kevin Keegan,
Oh what can it mean,
To a sad Geordie b*stard,
And a s*ite football team ...

Sit down, shut up,
Sit down, shut up,
Sit down, shut up,
Sit down, shut up,
Sit down, shut up ...

Shall we sing a,
Shall we sing a,
Shall we sing a song for you,
Shall we sing a song for you ...

We had joy,
We had fun,
We had Liverpool on the run,
But the fun didn't last coz the f**kers ran to fast ...

The babies not yours,
The babies not yours,
Oh Steven Gerrard,
The babies not yours ...

Oh we hate Bill Shankley and we hate St John, but most of all we hate Big Ron,

And we'll hang the Kopites one by one on the banks of the Royal Blue Mersey,

To Hell with Liverpool and Rangers too, throw them all in the Mersey,

And we'll fight fight fight with all our might for the boys in the Royal Blue Jersey,

Kopites are Gobsh*tes clap clap clap
Kopites are Gobsh*tes clap clap clap
Kopites are Gobsh*tes clap clap clap ...

It went quiet at Anfield Road,
Where we once watched us play with no strikers,
4 minutes to go,
Anichebe won a free kick,
Cahill put it in at the front stick,
It went quiet round the fields of Anfield Road ...
(Tune: Fields of Athenry)

Hark now hear,
The Everton Sing,
Liverpool ran away,
And we will fight for ever more,
Because of Derby Day ...

You are a farmer,
A dirty farmer,
Your only happy when making hay,
Your mums an info,
Your dads a scarecrow ,
So please don't take my tractor away

Are you Liverpool,

Are you Liverpool,

Are you Liverpool in disguise,

Are you Liverpool in disguise ...

Your sister is your mother,

Your father is your brother,

Your f*ckin one another,

The Derby family

Chelsea, Chelsea, wherever you may be,
You ain't got no history,
Lampard is fat,
Joe Cole is qu**r,
You ain't gonna win f**k all this year ...

One man couldn't carry (Carry)
Couldn't carry Lampard

One man and his forklift truck couldn't carry Lampard

Two men couldn't carry (Carry)
Couldn't carry Lampard

Two man one man and his forklift truck couldn't carry Lampard

Three men couldn't carry (Carry)
Couldn't carry Lampard

Three man, two man, one man and his forklift truck couldn't carry Lampard

(Continue Up To 10 Men)

Big Fat, Big Fat Frank
Big Fat, Big Fat Frank
Big Fat, Big Fat Frank
Big Fat Frankie Lampard

Build a bonfire,

Build a bonfire,

Put Liverpool on the top,

Put Arsenal in the middle,

And we'll burn the f*cking lot!

I've never felt more like singin' the blues,
When Everton win,
And Liverpool lose,
Oh Everton,
You got me singin' the blues ...

They're here,
They're there,
They're every f*cking where,
Empty seats, empty seats ...

F*ck all,
You've never won f*ck all
You've never won f*ck all
You've never won f*ck all

F*ck all,
You've never won f*ck all

Jingle bells,
jingle bells
jingle all the way
oh what fun it is to see Everton win away
Hey!
(Tune: Jingle Bells)

Stamford Bridge is falling down
Falling down, falling down
Stamford Bridge is falling down
Poor old Chelsea

Stand up if you hate Chelsea
Stand up if you hate Chelsea
Stand up if you hate Chelsea

Sit down if you hate Chelsea
Sit down if you hate Chelsea
Sit down if you hate Chelsea

Dance round if you hate Chelsea
Dance round if you hate Chelsea
Dance round if you hate Chelsea

Who, Who, Who, Who ...

(Sung when the other team makes a substitution and the players name is announced)

Dream on, Dream on,
With envy in your heart,
And you'll never with the league,
You'll never win the league - again, again, again ...

The Best Everton Football Chants Ever ...

Steve Gerrard, Gerrard,
He kisses the badge on his chest,
Then puts in a transfer request,
Steve Gerrard, Gerrard ...

You put your transfer in your transfer out,
In out in out you f*ck your club about,
You do the Stevie Gerrard and you change your mind,
That's what it's all about ...

If you hate Man United clap your hands,
If you hate Man United clap your hands,
If you hate Man United,
Hate Man United,
Hate Man United,
Clap your hands ...

Glory Hunters Man United!
Glory Hunters Man Untied!
Glory Hunters Man United!
Support Your Local Team!

The Best Everton Football Chants Ever ...

Chapter 4

*The referees a w*nker*

The Best Everton Football Chants Ever ...

Chapter 4 - *The referees a w*nker*

The referees a w*nker
The referees a w*nker
The referees a w*nker

Where's your Father?
Where's your Father?
Where's your Father, referee
you ain't got one
your a B*st*rd
your a B*st*rd referee

12 men …
You've only got 12 men …
You've only got 12 men …

12 men …
You've only got 12 men …
You've only got 12 men …

… The Best Everton Football Chants Ever …

Chapter 5

The Best Everton Websites

The Best Everton Football Chants Ever ...

Chapter 5 - *The Best Everton Websites*

Official Web Site:

www.evertonfc.com

Unofficial Web Sites:

www.toffeeweb.com

www.bluekipper.com

www.sos1878.co.uk

www.dixies60.com

www.everton-mad.co.uk

www.evertonresults.com

www.followeverton.com

www.evertoncollection.org.uk

www.followtonians.com

www.grandoldteam.com

www.toffeetalk.com

www.wsag.org

www.nsno.co.uk

www.606evertonians.com

www.clubeverton.co.uk

www.realevertonians.net

www.chuffedtobeblue.com

www.heysophie.wordpress.com

www.nilsatis1878.wordpress.com

www.peoplesblog.co.uk

Chapter 6

Everton Supporters Clubs

The Best Everton Football Chants Ever ...

Chapter 6 - Everton Supporters Clubs

www.evertonfc.com/membership-information.html

Aberdeen
Darren Cox   DCox4@slb.com

Aintree Blues
John Fitzpatrick   fitzefc@hotmail.com

Australia
Lee Sutherland   leesutherland@yahoo.com.au

Barrow in Furness
Peter Fell   fell140159@aol.com

Birkenhead
Joseph Wilson   joeywilson1@sky.com

Boston Evertonians
Ruairi Collins   bostonevertonians@gmail.com

Cape Town Toffees
Clinton Davids			davidsclinton@yahoo.com

Chorley Branch
Janet Carr			www.chorleytoffees.com

Coleraine Everton Supporters' Club
Gregory McDaid			gegs72@sky.com

Conwy
Bob Roberts			conwyefc@hotmail.co.uk

Cork
Kieran O'Sullivan			evertonfc.cork@yahoo.ie

Corner Pin Blues
Andrew Jones			stu-price@sky.com

Croxteth Blues
Paul Croft			crockyblues1963@yahoo.co.uk

Cumberland
Paul O'Leary			shadowglider@hotmail.com

Denbigh
Paul Evans   p.evans23@talktalk.net

Dublin
Dave Bergin   dbergin@eircom.ie

Elm Tree Supporters' Club
Louise Brown   luisay2m@yahoo.com

ESCL
AIan Critchley   www.escla.org.uk

Evertonians Thailand
Kasem Kiatsillapanan   pan_pan25@hotmail.com

Grimsby and Cleethorpes
davesearle2004@yahoo.co.uk

Han's Tours
Rachel Roberts   rach_eddie@hotmail.com

Harrogate & District
Diane Hilldiane   toffeegirl@btinternet.com

Helsby & Frodsham
Gary Cartwright   garycarty9@hotmail.com

Irish Toffees
Tom Maguire   blueboys@indigo.ie

Isle of Man
Juan Kermode   juankermode@hotmail.com

Lancaster & Morecambe
Andrew Balmer   abpunk@hotmail.co.uk

Mid Wales
Kurt Owen   midwalesevertonians@yahoo.co.uk

Midlands Area
Peter Owen   peter.owen16@live.co.uk

Milton Keynes
Tony Carson   tony.carson@btinternet.com

Netherton Blues
Gary Lambert   nethyblues@aol.com

The Best Everton Football Chants Ever …

North East
Rachel Flannery   rachel.flannery@newcastle.gov.uk

Northants
Rory Callinan   pukkaefc@hotmail.com

Northern Ireland
Peter Cross   escni.peter@btinternet.com

Old Swan Supporters
Alex Daley   gaz-efc@hotmail.com

Plymouth
Dave Roberts   dave.roberts@hotmail.co.uk

Polish Crew
Szymon Rokicki   szymonrokicki@gmail.com

Redditch
Tom Hill   tomhill.escra@btinternet.com

Rice Lane
James Lyon   j-lyon@sky.com

Russian Toffees
Pavel Kirillov   linard@mail.ru

Scottish Toffees
Tom Young   tom@totalstay.com

Shropshire Blues
Sean O'Flynn   sean.oflynn@gmail.com

South Coast Area
Dave Doherty   soblue@tiscali.co.uk

South Wales Branch
Mike Kempson   m.kempson3@ntlworld.com

Southport
Ian Munro   munrobluenose@aol.com

Southport Independent Blues
John Hughes   j-hughesl@tiscali.co.uk

Spain
Gordon Rowe   david_vickers@hotmail.co.uk

Swedish Toffees
Per Malm www.svenskafans.com/england/everton

Taxi Club Blues
Philip O'Rourkephil_ or@hotmail.com

Toronto Toffees
Allison Siddorn allisonsiddorn@yahoo.ca

Wakefield
Tracy White wakieblue@sky.com

Waterford, Ireland
David Fitzpatrick chevs@eircom.net

West Country Blues
Jackie Mounty jacquelm@jmounty.orangehome.co.uk

Widnes and Runcorn
Terry Seddon tdd.seddon@gmail.com

Wrexham
Anthony Clarke ktwood@toucansurf.com

The Best Everton Football Chants Ever ...

The Best Everton Football Chants Ever ...

We would like to thank everyone that has taken part in the book, and all those that have submitted material and features for the book.

If you would like to buy further copies please visit our website:

www.InterviewBooks.com/Everton.htm

Discounts are available for supporters clubs and associations.

If you would like to contribute new songs, chants or jokes for the next addition. Please email them to:

Everton@InterviewBooks.com

Printed in Great Britain
by Amazon.co.uk, Ltd.,
Marston Gate.